Midnight Memories

~ A Collection of Poetry & Prose ~

J. S. Brown

To my past –

Thank you for beating me down, so I could build myself back up again. Every broken heart I mended and every tear I wiped made me the woman I am today, the one with the confidence to write this book.

Table of Contents:

Part 1 – Depression & Anxiety

Inside Your Head

Have you been searching
For a meaning to this madness,
Running in circles
And drowning in sadness?
One day, you're hopeful,
And the next day, depressed.
When will you find happiness
Or refrain from being obsessed?
Is it entirely your fault
That you've lost your fight,
Because you don't reach for things,
Unless in your sight?
Are you lazy, anxious, and so tired
Of being this way?
Believe me, it will get better.
Just take it day-by-day.

Barely Waking Up in the Morning

Tired, of being tired.
No will, no drive,
No fight left inside.
Just settlements.
For a life you could be striving in,
But here you are, just barely surviving.

Prisoner of the Mind

Craving a life, you cannot achieve,
Is nothing more than agony.
"You can do anything you put your mind to,"
They tell you.
But what if your mind fears anything
That threatens to end
In heartache, betrayal, or defeat?
What if your mind confines your life
To this 12' by 12' room, locks the door,
And deliberately loses the key?

You must find the strength
To break down those walls.

Midnight Memories

It's midnight and I don't know how I got here.
I'm fine, physically, yet trembling with fear.
Anxiety always has a hold on me,
Stealing every ounce of courage that may be.

It's one-forty-five and I'm still awake.
My mind is racing. Sleep, I try to fake.
Why do I let myself sink so damn low?
With these demons inside, how will I grow?

It's three in the morning, tears are dry.
I'm slowly drifting, without a try.
Is this what it takes to calm the war?
Exhaustion can't be all I'm good for.

Living (Surviving)

Everything's crashing on the inside,
But the exterior is barely touched.
You've spent too long practicing a brave face,
And then crumbling when it's safe.

You're begging for someone
To help you live and not just survive.

I'm Not as Strong as I Thought I Was

I have reached the point
Where I can't acknowledge the pain,
I've lost so much, so many,
And I'm waiting for the gain.
I push the hurt aside,
Rubbing my temples
And slowing my breath.
When will this be over?
When will my demons reach their death?

The Spider's Web

I must change my perspective,
As the heart aches with confusion.
One day, I feel immense hate.
Yet others, the pain seems an illusion.

I constantly take for granted,
The wonderful life I possess.
Caught up in a selfish web
Of thoughts I cannot repress.

Hiding behind my excuses,
Wasting time and tears.
Becoming all too anxious
Over irrelevant fears.

Never having the confidence
Needed to do daily tasks.
Seen as weak by myself, and others.
"Help me," I'm unable to ask.

But the truth is:
You must never be afraid to ask for help.

Anxiety

Shaky hands,
Racing pulse,
Nervous twitch,
Never stops.

At the worst moments –
The most inconvenient times –
It holds me back.
It creates a fear

That I will mess up,
That I won't make it.
I want to stop,
I want control.

But control doesn't exist
When you're living
In fear that overwhelms,
No, envelopes.

I miss the days
When things were easy.
And forever won't be fun
With you on my back.

Wake the Living Inside Me

My words can cut like knives,
These thoughts could churn your belly.
I'm bottled up with no place to go.
As for my outlet, there's no telling

When I'll erupt to a boil,
Or simmer once I've cooked.
I'll wait for you to notice,
Yet I know you haven't looked.

Attention I mustn't beg for,
Respect; earned and not given.
But I'm screaming on the inside,
Praying for you to wake the living

From my frail bones,
As I'm too weak to carry on.
Yet every day I shake him off,
And tell the Devil: "so long!"

And then at night I see him,
Dancing in my dreams.
I could pinch myself and stop it all,
But I'm already awake, it seems.

I've Seen the Boogeyman

Dreams can be terrible realizations
Of the ugly person you've become.
The hurt you caused is laid in front of you,
And your darkest fears are wrapped up –
Waiting for you to make the wrong move.

You're sent into the oblivion of
Pain, sorrow, regret, and selfishness,
And you cannot call for help.
Darling, you're the one who started this fire.
How can you complain
About the flames you stoked?

After I've had a terrible dream,
My stomach is in knots
And I feel sick all day.

That's because I'm frightened
They will come true.

Depression

You're always going to be there,
Aren't you?
Lurking in the shadows.

You're always going to want me,
Aren't you?
Even when I've crushed you.

You're always going to come back,
Aren't you?
No matter how strong I am.

You're always going to haunt me,
Aren't you?
And I will be forced to succumb.

Paint Me a Perfect Life

Satisfaction is something
I haven't learned,
I'm always yearning for more.
Caught in between what I want
And what those want for me –
Painting a picture with my mind –
But I can't remember
Where I left my brushes.

My future is this canvas,
And all I see is a mess in front of me.

Doubts

Why did I choose this path,
Of which my legs can barely walk?
My mind is there,
But my soul is somewhere else

We're Only Human

I feel so angry today.
As if everyone
Is up against me.

I feel so shameful today.
Snapping on loved ones
And assuming the worst.

I feel so guilty today.
For putting myself
Through this pain.

I feel so human today.
So, I'll try my best
To do better tomorrow.

Under Water

And just like that –
The pain floods back in,
Surrounding me with it's cold embrace.
And the walls I built to keep me safe
Are now the reason I'm drowning
Because every time I patched a hole,
I fixed it up so fucking tight…

And now there's no room to breathe.

Lies I Tell Myself

I dig deep into myself,
Pulling out the darkest parts of me
And putting them on display,
Itching for an applause to echo
Through the silence in my head.

I don't need your approval.
I don't need your approval.
I don't need your approval.
This is what I tell myself.

But I beg for it anyway...

When Does "Adulthood" Start?

It's hard being young —
Growing into your skin,
Into yourself.

One day everything is so scary.
And then somehow, you figure it out.
But do you ever really *figure it out?*

The Little Boat (Part 1)

Tell me, do you have the anecdote,
For the thirst that burns inside my throat?
A longing for some safety,
And really, you can't blame me.
When you're the one who made me
So damn cold, and afraid.
Trust me, I don't want to feel this way.
But every time I numb the pain
I wake up and it's there the next day.
And I wonder if I'll ever really be okay
With this feeling in my throat.
When I'm just a little boat,
Cast into your violent sea –
One that keeps drowning me.

Don't Get Caught Up in the Lies You Spit

How many lies will you tell them,
Before they finally give up on you?

How many lies will you tell yourself,
Before you forget who you really are?

The Anxious Haiku

Why do I let fear
Leave me swollen, stranded here?
Let me disappear.

Rage

How do you choose
Not to be angry
Over something
You cannot change?
Something,
You cannot control?

Let Down Those Walls

I know the numbness you feel
Is an envelope protecting you
From the pain that lurks outside –
It wraps you up and keeps you warm.
But does it really protect you
When you can't feel anything at all?

Solitude

Don't worship me,
For I have sinned.
And all my lies
Blow in the wind.
The face you see,
This mask I hold,
Will always hide the
Nightmares I've told.
So, turn away
And slam the door,
Silence is what
I came here for.

Making Friends

These monsters run wild inside of me,
Because I let them.
Sometimes, when I get lonely,
They take my hand
And we dance together.

The Devil's Apprentice

The Devil's in my head
And he won't let me rest
Despite all his flaws,
I give him my best.
To others, I'm a monster,
To him – a coward.
I'm a slave to his wishes,
As I give him all this power.
Tell me, will I ever
Be free of these chains?
Or will I continue
On this path of blood stains?

Part 2 – Heartache & Grief

Settling for Restlessness

The love.
The energy.
All the greatness
I have inside me is wasted,
On those with too small of minds
To challenge this wild soul.

Your Broken Heart

Walk your broken heart through that door,
I can't watch your pain anymore.
You've lost all the light in your eyes.
I've seen your struggles, heard your cries.

Walk your broken heart through that door,
This can't be all you're living for.
You're far too young to feel like this,
Your vibrant soul, I have missed.

Walk your broken heart through that door,
You're not done living, no, there's more.
We'll fix you, together, my friend.
I will not let this be your end.

Come Back to Me

I hope you hurt more than I do,
But that's a lie because I don't.
I want you to be okay, happy even,
Yet I can't help but feel used.

Sometimes when I think of you
My heart wants to leap from beneath
My ribs, but I won't let it.
I suppress everything.

I've become almost professional,
At pushing the feelings aside, away, afar.
It's not hard at all, in fact,
It's a chore to feel anything at all.

But who am I fooling?
It's 2am and I'm crying out
Your name on the bathroom floor.
Please come back to me, don't leave forever.

Beautiful Crash

I crashed today when you crept into my
mind. Like a wave hitting the shore, I saw
you coming, still, I was unprepared. I don't
believe I will ever swallow this pain. Just the
sound of your name strikes my heart in such
a way that I can't breathe. When will I learn
to cope with you being gone? Living has
never been easy but, living without you is
unbearable.

I crashed today when I found your picture
and my knees became weaker than the day
you left me. I'm an adult and I couldn't keep
myself composed. I think it feels good to
grieve you, as horrible as that sounds. I've
spent way too long blocking the pain out
and sometimes it feels beautiful to let go of it
all.

Falling Out of Love

We were smiling ear to ear,
But now we only fake it.
You used to be my goodnight kiss,
But now we don't even bother.
Activities we shared fell through the cracks,
When spending time with one another
Became a chore.
I'll take the blame because
I know you see the end too.
I won't hurt you because,
We're bigger than that.

Your Memory

I'm okay with missing you today.
At least I know I'm still thinking
About my unconditional love for you.
I fear the day you stop running
Through my dreams because
I never want to let you go.

Drinking & Driving Kills

What's it going to take?
For you to smarten up,
And put the bottle down.

What's it going to take?
For you to consider the outcomes
And consequences of your actions.

Who do you have to lose?
Before you think twice
About getting behind the wheel.

Who do you have to lose?
Before you understand
How selfish it all is.
How many more?
Until you remember
How you got here.

All it took was one stop sign.
What you lost was your best friend
And now you'll never have
"Just one more," of anything at all.

I Don't Want to Be Like You

How does it make you feel to know
How broken you've made me?
How do you sleep,
Fully aware of the piece of shit
That you truly are?
I love you enough to look past it
But it's hard to know when
"Turning a blind eye,"
Becomes only plain stupidity.

Aftermath

Maybe I like the conflict because
At least it keeps you close to me,
But now it's the only thing
Keeping us apart
And sometimes,
I just wish I knew what I wanted.
Then, I'd be able to hold on to you,
No sweaty palms.

But when the dust settles,
I feel restless, time and time again.
Yet how can I use that as an excuse?
There will be another storm
And the dust will settle again.

Will you pick up the pieces
In the aftermath of yourself?
Or will you run away
Like you've done so before?

Tu Me Manques

In the language of French,
One says: *"tu me manques,"*
Which means, "you are missing from me."
These words are a perfect portrayal
Of my emotions about you being gone.
A part of me was taken when
You left this world behind.
A part of me is missing,
I believe that part is you.

I've Never Felt This Broken

The worst pain one can feel,
Is losing due to your own failures.
It may sound foolish, but trust me,
Having someone to blame makes
Grieving so much easier.

<u>Is It Over?</u>

They say bad things
Always come in threes
And today I really hope that's true.
Because this life has
Brought me to my knees,
If only you'd seen what I've been through.

Please, Let This Be a Dream

I've screamed
I've cried, and oh
Have I hurt.
I just was not ready for this pain.
But who am I kidding?
No one can truly prepare
For losing a piece of themselves.

Shattered Openings

They say, "the eyes are the windows to your soul," and I've been leaving the windows open trying to let the breeze in. It's been really dark in here and I needed to feel the light.

Keeping the curtains open gets hard when the rain feels so heavy. Sometimes, terrible things pass by my windows and I fight to refrain from drawing the curtains.

You see, these windows are my eyes – the opening to my soul – and with every terror that passes by, my openings become a little more shattered.

Mama

How ironic is it that –
I have so many questions for
The woman I should know
Like the back of my hand?

I watched you pretend to be
Someone else, my whole life.
Maybe that's why
You feel like a stranger.

The Positive Side of Heartbreak

This feeling will end.
Pain – only temporary.
Break, so you can mend.

I Care Too Much

My empathy
Tends to drain me
Of all the energy I own.

Guardian Angel

This pain I feel only proves
How endless my love for you is.
It validates the memories,
Softens the tears.
Until the day we meet again,
I'll watch for you in the clouds.

<u>Broken Family</u>

They say, "blood is thicker than water," so
how come my blood never carried me as far
as the river could?

You were supposed to be my guide against
the current, but somehow, you became the
anchor weighing me down.

Lost Soul

I'm unsure of the direction
For which I want to take.
A lost soul: I have been for so long.
But trust me, it's my mistake.

I've burned every bridge,
Tore down every door.
A little bit of happiness
Was all I yearned for.

But now, I wander lonely –
Anxious with every turn –
To be stuck in the shadows,
Unable to grow, afraid to learn.

My Indestructible Heart

I picked the broken pieces up off the floor
and stuffed them in my pockets. I wasn't
going to let you lose any more parts; shatter
any more fragments. So, I tucked them away
as quickly as I could. Meanwhile, you
laughed at my sad attempt to salvage
something that's been cracked so many
times. I hid my tears with my long hair, as I
hung my head as low as my neck could bear.
In that moment, I wanted to melt into the
carpet and disappear forever. When you
slammed the door leaving, it woke me from
my misery and I scrambled to fix myself,
once again. With every tear and every hope,
I put my heart back together again. And this
time, I will never let you break it.

Catch Me If You Can

I've been dancing in the shadows,
Where you will never find me.

The Heartache of Growing Up

Take me back to the days
When crawling underneath the sheets
Made all the monsters disappear.
Take me back to the moments
When Grandma's kisses healed
Every wound, every broken heart.
I miss the days when
Your brother was
The biggest bully you knew,
And you loved him fiercely.
I miss the days when
Things were less complicated
And a simple "Dear Diary"
Solved every fear.

Can You Hear Me?

Losing you
Left me so angry.
So, I've been howling
At the moon and hoping,
That wherever you may be,
You can hear me crying out for you.

You'll Need Antibiotics After Loving Me

Sometimes I get so overwhelmed
And I lose myself completely.
The anger can pour from my limbs
Faster than the Spring rainfall.
When I'm aware of my actions,
I watch myself tear apart
The people I love,
With my words.

My tongue can cut
The deepest wounds,
And I've never learned
How to heal the infections
That I seem to cause.
The skin just builds up
Over time – gets thicker.
But then I'm back again
To rip it back open.

Your scabs will never smooth over until
you've rid me of your life.

Part 3 – Love & Commitment

Love at First Sight

When we meet, stars will collide.
The Earth will shift,
The Moon will swallow the Sun.

When we touch,
Everything we know will disintegrate.
And the new world which we created,
Will be ours, to adventure and grow in.

And even without the Sun,
We're never in the darkness.
Because the only light we need
Burns bright in our chests.

Let's Try Again Tomorrow

Let my soul rest,
Turn off the lights.
It's been a long year and
I'm tired of these fights.

You won't change,
But God knows I have.
I don't recognize us and
I'm unsure of this path.

We both have our flaws,
And time is not to borrow.
So, let's take a break for now,
And try to love tomorrow.

Commitment

Commitment; easier said than done.
In the beginning, we put our all into it,
Soaking up every ounce of peace it brings us.

We often forget that commitments
Big or small, can be eternal when
Commitments involve the hearts of others.

Life is short, but can feel so long
When spent with the wrong person.
Commitment; easier said than done.

Some of the Things I Love About You

I love sliding into bed next to you,
Where I fit perfectly.

When you are at peace,
I feel complete.

I love wrapping myself around your skin,
Listening to every heartbeat.

This world has been far from kind to you,
And I wish I could soften it all.

I love the sounds that escape from you,
As you sleep your stress away.

We have our battles; we have our triumphs.
I love you, and all of it, unconditionally.

<u>Your Eyes</u>

I see a thousand memories
Behind your eyes,
Some past, and some future.

I see a house,
A healthy family,
And so much happiness.

I see you and me,
Against the world,
Against everything.

I see mistakes,
I see tears.
But I also see laughter.

I see two humans
Building a beautiful life,
Despite all odds.

I see a whole lot more than colour
When I look into your eyes.
I see us, forever.

Run Away with Me

What have you done to me?
Your eyes are all I see when I close mine.
I don't know how to go on,
I'm no longer on a straight line.

Meet me in the auburn of morning,
And run away with me.
We can kill our pasts and start anew,
Let's go somewhere and be free.

Attachments

Sometimes we attach ourselves
To people and things around us.
At first, it seems so beautiful,
But age can wither beauty.

Stolen kisses soon become
A dream you only see at dawn.
And the passion that once burned bright,
Now waits to be stoked once more.

That's why space can be healthy,
And space can save so much pain.
You can't expect to latch on
To someone's life without resent.

You must carve your own path
And continue to dig ditches,
Until you find your way home
Then you may attach to someone.

Because only then will there be nothing to
lose.

Their Distance is for Safety Precautions

She's gotten good at suppressing him, yet
every now and then she catches herself
slipping from reality and into something she
knows damn well is no good for her. He's
covered in flags of past lovers' blood, yet
something entices her, invites her, excites
her. She's never been a decision-maker and I
guess that's why she keeps him far enough
away, so the sparks don't ignite their bones
on fire.

I Wish I Didn't Need You

I've been busy making homes out of people
when I should have been making a home
out of myself. You can't expect someone to
keep you safe and warm if you don't know
how to do it for yourself. It took me so long
to realize that you get what you give. I'm so
sorry, I've been expecting you to love me
harder than I can love you.

I will try harder, every day to be the woman
you deserve — to make a home out of us —
but more importantly, to become so strong
that I don't need you. Because I will always
want you but, I need to learn to live without
you anyways.

Your Voice

Your voice sends shivers through me,
Especially when you say my name.
Sometimes I imagine your lips on mine,
And suddenly, I can't breathe.
Love is such a fragile thing,
Yet every day I am so careless with it.
Dreaming of you, but afraid to jump
Is so unfair to both of us.

Stubborn

The attention you give,

Is all I've ever wanted.

But I'm so good at being stubborn,

Why give it all away now?

The tease is where the fun lies.

And I'm having such a good time

Running circles around your heart,

That I've forgotten my way back to you.

You deserve someone willing to chase you

Until your breathless and drunk on love –

From the beginning of your love

To the ends of the earth and back again.

Loving You

Loving you was never easy

But that doesn't mean it wasn't worth it.

Loving you was never simple,

But that doesn't mean I didn't enjoy it.

Loving you made me crazy,

Yet so does this whole world.

Loving you made me sad,

Yet so do rainy days.

Loving you involved decisions

Ones I shouldn't have had to make.

Loving you carried sacrifices,

Ones I shouldn't have contemplated.

And as much as I hated you,

You must know how much I loved you.

And you must accept that we're moving on.

Connections

Everyone has different relationships
With the souls around them.
Sometimes I find myself feeling
Jealous of other people's connections.
But I fail to realize the own
Connections I create with others.
Just because I don't light you
Up the way they do
Doesn't mean I don't light
You up at all, dear.
If she's your daytime,
I can be your night.
We all hold different things
Inside ourselves, different assets
To donate to those around you.

Missed You While I Was Sleeping

I missed you while I was sleeping,

As crazy as that sounds,

I was hoping to see you tonight,

In a dream that knows no bounds.

You could call me clingy.

But I think I'm just in awe –

Of everything you are my dear,

I'll love your every flaw.

Never Letting Go

Growing up,

Growing apart.

Learning life,

Learning about each other.

Too young to be perfect,

To have it figured out.

But even when it gets hard,

The last thing I want to do,

Is give up.

Love Storm

Lay beside me.

Let my ocean

Wash waves of love

Over your tired soul.

Collide with me.

And when the tide

Pulls you out,

Come back to me.

Find heaven in me.

Lay all your worries

On the floor,

With our clothes.

Climb and fall around me.

Together, we make

Lightning crash, thunder roar –

A beautiful, sensual storm

Fortunate to Be Able to Love

How fortunate am I
To have legs to carry me,
Hands to hold you,
And a mouth to show you
Just how much I care.

I Don't Want to Live Without You

If something were to happen,

Would you meet me, in my dreams?

I know, it's hard to think about.

But we're not immortal it seems.

Never Settle for Less Than You Deserve

Her hair was long,

But her patience was not.

His arms were strong,

But the man's heart was weak.

And she would never settle for him.

Lover/Dreamer

The first time I held your hand,
I had the urge to grab it tight
And run away to the depths
Of our wildest dreams.
I got caught up in the wonder
Of your endless eyes.
And even after all these years,
They still keep me dreaming.

True Love

Someday, we'll be wiser
And will finally be able to see
That I was made for you
And you were made for me.

Sure About You

I'm not confident
In anything that I do,
Except loving you.

Your Smile

That smile you beam

From cheek, to cheek,

Has such a way of

Leaving me weak.

You're my Fairy Tale

Stick yourself in a book, so I can read you. I want to know where you came from. Did you know your parents – your grandparents? Who tucked you in at night? Tell me all the questions you never got to ask. And when I've finished reading you, I hope to be in your sequel.

Thank You for Helping Me Grow

You plant flowers in the darkest parts of me
And then you bathe me in your light.

Part 4 – Happiness & Inspiration

One Day

One day, you will be so happy that your heart will burst from your chest.

One day, you will be so free that your legs won't keep you on the ground anymore.

One day, you will finally open the chapter that leads to healing.

One day, the indecisiveness won't eat you up anymore.

One day, you won't be so anxious about the things you didn't do.

One day, nothing will stop you from achieving your dreams.

One day, the one you need will be there waiting for you.

One day, the uncertainty won't be so heavy anymore.

One day, the steps you take won't feel so small.

One day, you will finally live, and oh, how beautiful it's going to feel.

I'm Growing Up, OK?

At just eighteen years,

I realized some things.

Unsure of myself,

Going nowhere fast,

I was overwhelmed.

Driving through the snow,

Screaming to music,

I told myself that

"You're doing just fine."

Realization came.

It's okay if you

Feel hopeless as fuck.

It's okay if you

Change your mind, again.

But promise me, please, that you'll be happy.

Changes

It's okay to change.

Change is inevitable,

So why shouldn't we embrace it?

You're going to spend

Over 50 years in

This fucking place.

Adapt to challenges.

Grow in time.

Heal with knowledge.

You're going to make it,

One way or another,

One day at a time.

Acceptance

Sometimes, I can't breathe,

Because it all seems too much.

How do you find control

When you have no idea what you want?

How do you choose one option

Out of a sea of millions?

I've spent years overthinking,

Sulking, hurting, healing, and changing.

Losing friends and loved ones

On this painful journey.

I've wasted sleep, tears, and memories

On this monster inside me.

It's been half a decade

And I haven't come to terms with who I am

Small Doses of Happiness

And it's moments like these

That show me why I am alive.

A sense of purpose shines through the cracks,

But I'm incapable of remembering it

When I need it most.

Conquer

The hardest decisions

Have the most beautiful outcomes.

In the beginning, you're stricken with fear,

Replaying every possible scenario

In your head,

So, you can attempt to make sense of it all.

But you will never make sense

Of something you cannot perceive.

You see, anything could happen.

The smallest circumstances

Can alter everything.

Instead of waiting, wondering, and hurting,

Push through the fear. and just do it!

What's the worst that could happen?

Nothing more than what you could handle.

You were made to conquer mountains.

Life Is A Gift

This is a big world
It holds 7 billion hearts,
Dreams, secrets, souls.

We often forget
The actual size of
Our problems and sorrows.

Compared to others,
Some have it golden.
Still, they cry themselves to sleep.

Why are we so quick
To assume we have it bad?
Every breath you take is a gift.

Stop for a second, listen to your heartbeat.
Be grateful that you are alive today.

Don't Judge A Woman by Her Cover

Women are weak,

Because we care.

Women are a bitch,

Because we're told not to care.

Women are sensitive,

Because we've been through hell.

Women are crazy,

Because we were told not to react.

I shouldn't have to apologize,

For having a heart filled with love.

I shouldn't have to apologize,

For having fears, anxieties, and values.

I shouldn't have to apologize,

For having an opinion on my life.

I shouldn't have to apologize,

For being a strong, empowered woman.

Crash & Burn

Every person has multiple faces.

They have the one they love,

The one they hate.

There's the one used to impress

And the one used for innocence.

Everyone has a face that creeps

Out uncontrollably

Or the one they're trying to change

The point is, we're all trying

To be something, someone

So, pick a face and try it out.

If you crash and burn its fine.

Because this is just a small part

Of the enormous role

You play in this game of life.

Time

Time can move so quick when you're desperately trying to hold on to a moment that you never want to forget.

Sometimes, you skip being grateful and dive right into the joy. Suddenly, the moment is over, and life pulls you back down again.

Time can drag on, and on when you're anxious and your brain won't conclude a goddamn thing.

Time moves slow when you're barely 20 – a couple just trying to make ends meet – yet it can move so fast when you're married and in the blink of an eye there's a baby.

My advice is to stop counting the minutes and start counting the moments. The truth is: time will never stop. It's your job to make every second count.

Don't Need Nobody

You must learn to love yourself
In every possible way you could want.
No one is going to give you the love
You think you deserve.
Don't you know how hard people fight
Every day, just to love themselves?
What on earth makes you so special?

Choose Your Garden

I don't think you realize

All the potential your past left you with.

Yes, you've crawled through hell

And reached the light,

But that doesn't mean

You can wipe your hands clean and be done.

All the bullshit you've endured

Can shape you into quite the man,

If you absorb the knowledge,

Instead of expecting sympathy for your hardships.

We all pick the garden in which we choose to grow.

Why did you stay in the ashes

When you could have thrived in the sunlight?

Perspective

But what if it's not about

The way the world looks at you,

But more, the way you look at it?

Falling in Love with Life

A perfect day

Involves making my own choices –

Throw a little adventure in!

With the wind in my hair,

A smile plastered across my cheeks,

And a heart so full of wonder,

I'll never stop learning

How to love being alive.

Just Let the Light In

The box you're in feels so dark
And heavy, but one day
The light will shine through.
You will lift it off and see the Sun
Cleaning all your sins away.

A Dream for You

I dream of

Feeding you life,

Instead of pain

And nutrients,

Instead of toxicity.

The Little Boat (Part 2)

Once there was a little boat

In an ocean much bigger than he.

The waves were strong,

But still he rowed on.

There were so many places to see!

Shine Your Light

How do you shine a light
On someone who
Only knows darkness?
How can I convince you
That it's not about who's
Gone the farthest?
Will you ever realize that
You don't always have
To be the hardest?
Will you continue to
Shine your light,
Even on the heartless?

Phoenix Rising

I just wanted to tell you

How powerful you really are.

From the ashes, you rose,

Even when the flames surrounded you.

All the hands that held you down,

Now make up the armor you wear.

Just like I knew you always were –

The Phoenix Rising.

Break the Chains

It doesn't matter how far you run

When you're running from yourself.

You can't escape a past that's

Always so close behind you.

When something attaches itself to you –

Whether it be a memory or a person –

It can be nearly impossible to break free.

The grasp your trauma can have on you

Can be tighter than you can bear,

But that doesn't mean you'll never be free.

One can learn to break the chains

They're bound by, however,

It takes quite some time –

The deepest wounds always do.

The Hidden Truth

The hidden truth

You've been searching for,

Lies in all the places

You're too afraid to look.

Open your eyes.

Test Your Strength

Can I tell you a secret?
You are going to be someone great –
The brightest star in the sky.

Getting there won't be easy,
But you already did the hardest part:
The first step, well, let's call it a stumble.

You've always been a rebel at heart,
Unwilling to play it safe yet,
Afraid to make a mistake,

You could scream for guidance but,
Who would listen?
You've cried wolf so many times,
And now it's your turn
To fight the bloody battles.

You're afraid of the moments

In between this small town,

And where you're supposed to be.

But oh, how exciting the uncertainty is

When safety is all you've ever known?

You'll never learn to fly if you don't take any leaps.

So, drive a truck through your heart

To see what happens.

You'll never know your strength,

If you don't test its limits.

I've Come So Far

I remember when

I hated waking up

In the morning.

Now, I can't wait

To feel the Sun

Touch my pale skin.

I used to fight

Myself to sleep.

And these days,

I'm so exhausted

From the simple

Act of living.

Be Proud

Has it been hard
Staying strong,
When you've been
Practicing for so long?

You should be so proud
Of whom you are today.
It takes a lot of courage,
To play the part you play.

You've seen it all,
Through weep and fears
And never let it change you,
Even after all these years.

Just Be Happy

You can ruin
So many moments,
Wasting time
Being sad.

With that,
My final note to you
Is to *just be happy*.

Acknowledgements:

To the Reader –

Thank you for reading the words of my heart and soul. They wouldn't mean half as much without you here to read them! I sincerely hope they spoke to you in an indescribable way – that's what I write for.

From the bottom of my heart, thank you so much for finding a place in your life (and hopefully on your shelf) for _Midnight Memories!_

Find more work by the author on Instagram:
_@jsbrown_poetry_

To Edison –

Thank you for so many beautiful years, and for telling people your girl was an author – long before I ever believed in myself, or my writing. You are absolutely everything to me, and this book would not have been completed without your encouragement.

To Papa –

Every ounce of knowledge in my brain all roots back to you, thank you for teaching me all that I know. Since I was a little girl, you have always been my biggest fan and I am determined to make you unbelievably proud of me!

To Dad –

The love between a father and daughter is a unique and special bond. My whole life you've been my protector, always working yourself to the bone so I had clothes on my back and food in my stomach. Although we don't always see eye-to-eye, the love we share will never wither. Thank you for making me the fierce, opinionated, and intelligent woman I am today!

Printed in Great Britain
by Amazon